Essential Physical Science

ROCKS AND MINERALS

Chris Oxlade

Heinemann
LIBRARY

Chicago, Illinois

© 2014 Heinemann Library
an imprint of Capstone Global Library, LLC
Chicago, Illinois

To contact Capstone Global Library, please
call 800-747-4992, or visit our web site,
www.capstonepub.com

Edited by Andrew Farrow and Abby Colich
Designed by Cynthia Akiyoshi
Original illustrations © Capstone Global Library
    Ltd 2014
Illustrated by HL Studios
Picture research by Tracy Cummins
Originated by Capstone Global Library Ltd
Printed in China by China Translation and
    Printing Services

17 16 15 14 13
10 9 8 7 6 5 4 3 2

**Library of Congress Cataloging-in-Publication
Data**
Oxlade, Chris.
  Rocks and minerals / Chris Oxlade.
     p. cm.—(Essential physical science)
  Includes bibliographical references and index.
  Summary: "The Earth's rocks and minerals are
incredibly varied, but they have many features in
common. This book explores the main types of
rocks, looking at their characteristics, properties,
and uses"--Provided by publisher.
  ISBN 978-1-4329-8150-1 (hb)—ISBN 978-1-4329-
8159-4 (pb)
  1. Petrology—Juvenile literature. 2. Minerals—
Juvenile literature. I. Title.

QE432.2.O953 2014
552—dc23   2012046878

Acknowledgments
We would like to thank the following for
permission to reproduce photographs: Capstone
Library: pp. 14 (Karon Dubke), 15 (Karon Dubke),
18 (Karon Dubke), 19 (Karon Dubke), 30 (Karon
Dubke), 31 (Karon Dubke); Getty Images: pp. 13
(Carsten Peter/Speleoresearch & Films); 20 (Alan
Majchrowicz), 21 (Ed Reschke), 25 (Dave Hamman),
28 (G. R. 'Dick' Roberts/NSIL), 32 (Ed Reschke), 35
(Jason Edwards); Photo Researches: pp. 10 (Phillip
Hayson), 11 (Charles D. Winters / Science Source);
Shutterstock: pp. 4 (© kojihirano), 5 (© scyther5), 7
(© PavelSvoboda), 9 (© beboy), 17 (© Qing Ding),
22 (© VLADJ55), 23 (© Ronald Sumners), 26 (©
Katrina Brown), 27 (© berna namoglu), 37 (© Patryk
Kosmider), 40 (© Offscreen), 41 (© Manamana), 42
(© John Copland); Superstock: pp. 16 (Brad Lewis /
Science Faction), 29 (Universal Images Group), 34
(Louie Psihoyos / Science Faction), 36 (DeAgostini),
39 (PhotoAlto), 43 (Cubo Images).

Cover photographs of pebbles reproduced with
permission from Superstock (Westend61).

Contents

Eureka moment!

Learn about important discoveries that have brought about further knowledge and understanding.

DID YOU KNOW?

Discover fascinating facts about rocks and minerals.

WHAT'S NEXT?

Read about the latest research and advances in essential physical science.

Some words are shown in bold, **like this**. You can find out what they mean by looking in the glossary.

What Are Rocks and Minerals?

You are never very far from a rock! Standing on the Earth's surface, there are usually rocks a few yards below your feet. Rocks form the surface of the Earth, and continue down into the Earth for many miles.

There are many different types of rock. You might have heard of some of them. How about sandstone, marble, or granite? If you haven't heard of them, you almost certainly have seen them. In many places, such as mountains and coasts, rocks are exposed at the Earth's surface. We also see them in homes and around town, as many buildings are constructed from rock. Materials such as **gravel** and sand are made up of particles of rock.

These amazing red, orange, and white towers of sandstone rocks can be seen in the Bryce Canyon National Park in Utah.

Minerals

Minerals are the materials that make up rocks. A mineral is a solid, nonliving material. Most rocks are made up of a few different minerals mixed together. Quartz and feldspar are two of the most common minerals.

Rocks and minerals play an important role in our lives. As well as being a useful building material, rocks are a source of metals and precious stones such as diamonds. And we use minerals in many products, from **concrete** to toothpaste.

This ring is made from three materials found in rocks — the metal gold, and the precious stones diamonds and sapphires.

What's Inside the Earth?

If you could dig a hole through the Earth, you would discover that the rocks we see at the surface of the Earth only make up a thin **crust** on the outside of the Earth. All the rocks we talk about in this book are in the crust. Under the crust you would find very thick layers of rock, before reaching the center of the Earth.

Peeling the Earth

The main layers of the Earth are the crust, the mantle, and the core. Under the Earth's **continents** the crust is about 30 miles (50 kilometers) thick. There is also crust under the oceans, but here it is thinner—between 3 miles (5 kilometers) and 6 miles (10 kilometers) thick. The crust is very thin compared to the size of the Earth, which is 7,926 miles (12,756 kilometers) across. You can think of it as being like the skin on an apple.

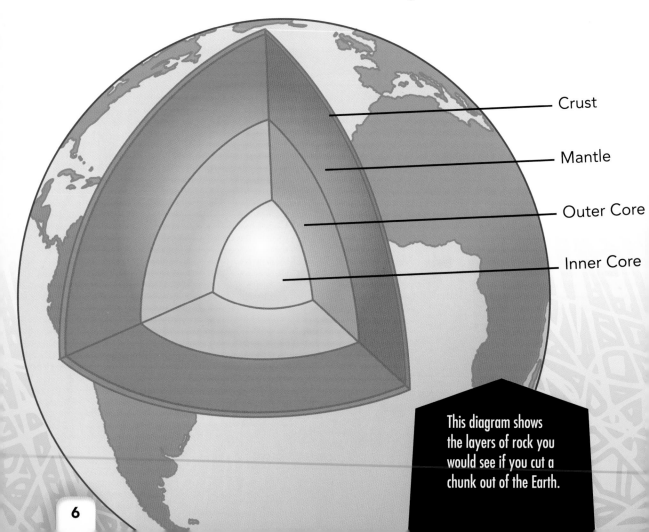

Crust

Mantle

Outer Core

Inner Core

This diagram shows the layers of rock you would see if you cut a chunk out of the Earth.

Under the crust is the mantle, which is the thickest layer of the Earth. Under the mantle, in the center of the Earth, is the core. The rocks get hotter as you move toward the center of the Earth. Right in the center, the temperature is 8,500°F (4,700°C) or above.

DID YOU KNOW?

In some places on the Earth there are very hot rocks very close to the surface. This is often where there are volcanoes. A geyser is a spectacular natural fountain of boiling water caused by these rocks. When water flows down cracks into the rocks, it quickly boils, making steam. The steam blasts water back out of the cracks, making a fountain.

Tectonic plates

The crust (that's the thin, outer layer of the Earth) is broken into pieces called **tectonic plates**. Some are thousands of miles across, while others are just hundreds of miles across. Some plates are made up of thicker continental crust, some of thinner oceanic crust, and some of both kinds of crust.

This map shows the world's major tectonic plates. The jagged lines are where the plates are moving apart. The smooth lines are where they are colliding.

The **tectonic plates** are moving, but very, very slowly. Even the quickest plates move at only about 4 inches (10 cm) in a year, but over millions of years they move thousands of miles. Millions of years ago the continents were in different places from where they are today, and millions of years from now the continents will be in completely new positions.

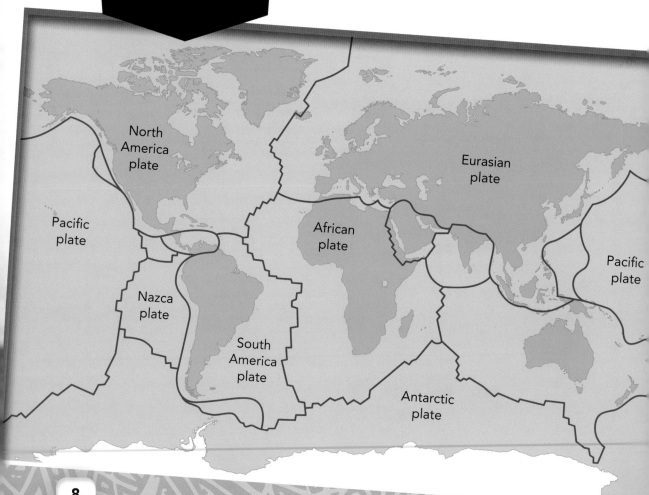

North America plate

Eurasian plate

Pacific plate

African plate

Pacific plate

Nazca plate

South America plate

Antarctic plate

At the edges

The places where one plate meets another are called **plate boundaries**. In some places the edges of the plates are moving apart. As they do, molten rock (called **magma**) rises from underneath the crust to fill the gap. In other places plates are moving toward each other. Their edges scrunch together and one plate slides down under the other. At these plate boundaries new rocks are formed and old rocks are changed.

Eureka!

Alfred Wegener (1880-1930) was a German scientist who realized that the coastlines of South America and Africa fit together like two pieces of a jigsaw puzzle. He suggested that the Earth's continents are slowly moving around. About 250 million years ago all the continents were joined together in one giant continent, which he called Pangaea.

Where tectonic plates move apart, molten rock sometimes reaches the surface, forming a volcano. When the lava cools, it forms new rock.

What Minerals Are There?

Minerals are made up of chemical **elements** joined together. For example, the mineral calcite is made up of the **elements** calcium, carbon, and oxygen, and the mineral quartz is made up of the elements silicon and oxygen. A few minerals are made up of just one element. For example, gold contains only the element gold, and diamond contains only carbon. Geologists divide minerals into groups depending on the elements they contain.

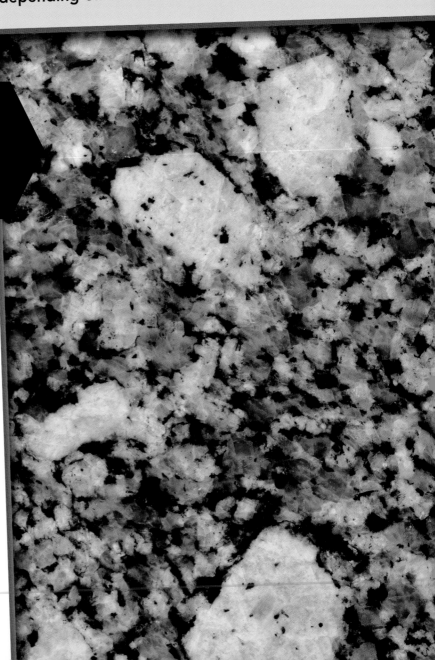

This is a close-up picture of a type of rock called granite. The light-colored minerals are quartz and feldspar. The dark minerals are mica and hornblende.

Common minerals

There are thousands of different minerals in the Earth's rocks, but most rocks are made up of just a few minerals. The most common minerals found in rocks include feldspar, quartz, mica, and olivine. Feldspar is most common. It makes up about half of all rocks.

The properties of minerals

Geologists describe minerals by their properties. These properties include color, lustre (whether they are dull or shiny), and transparency (how much light can shine through them). They also include hardness. This is tested using a scale called Moh's scale, which goes from 1 (very soft) to 10 (very hard). To find out the hardness of a mineral, the mineral is tested to see if it scratches a mineral of known hardness. Another important property is the shape of a mineral's **crystals** (see pages 12 and 13).

WHAT'S NEXT?

Geologists have discovered about 3,800 minerals in the Earth's crust. Each year they discover dozens more. Many minerals are useful for manufacturing things from concrete to electronic components. In the future we will probably find more minerals we can put to good use.

An assortment of minerals are found in rocks, including silver, sulfur, sapphire, fluorite, ruby, galena, copper, beryl, malachite, and azurite.

Crystals

Minerals are made up of particles, which are atoms or groups of atoms. In nearly all minerals the particles are arranged in neat, three-dimensional rows and columns, so they are neatly packed together. Materials with their particles arranged like this are called crystals.

One way that crystals form is when water that has minerals dissolved in it **evaporates**. As the water evaporates, the particles of the mineral join together, and a crystal begins to grow. Crystals grow with flat faces and straight edges. This is evidence that the particles are neatly arranged.

Mineral crystals also form when molten rock cools and turns to a solid. You can easily see these crystals in some types of rock, such as granite. The particles in mineral crystals are neatly arranged, but they don't have straight edges and flat faces you can see because each crystal is joined to the next.

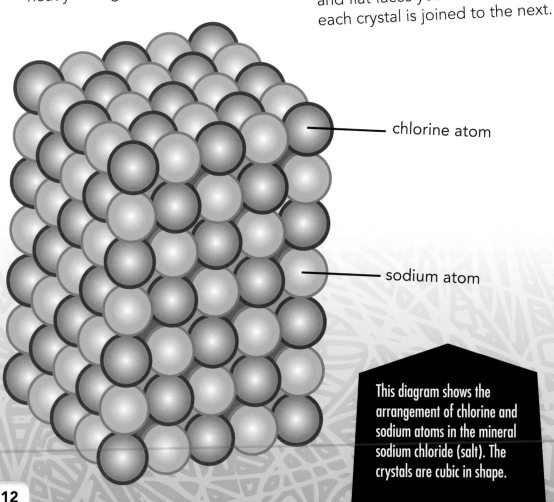

chlorine atom

sodium atom

This diagram shows the arrangement of chlorine and sodium atoms in the mineral sodium chloride (salt). The crystals are cubic in shape.

Crystal shapes

Different minerals have different shapes of crystals, with different numbers of faces and edges. Crystal shapes include cubic, which has six faces like a box, and hexagonal, which is like a cylinder with six faces around the outside.

Massive selenite crystals dwarf an explorer (dressed in orange in the back of the cave) in the amazing Cave of Crystals in northern Mexico.

Try This!

The minerals in rocks are normally in crystal form. Try this to grow your own crystals of the mineral magnesium sulfate (known as epsom salts).

Prediction

Crystals that grow freely (not in a confined space) will have straight edges and flat faces because their particles will join up in neat rows and columns.

Equipment

- epsom salts (You can obtain this from a pharmacist. An adult will have to buy it for you.)
- cup
- teaspoon
- dish
- magnifying glass

Ask an adult to help you with this experiment.

What you do

1 Boil some water in a kettle, then fill a cup with hot water.

2 Add a teaspoon of epsom salts to the water and stir to make the powder dissolve. Keep adding powder a teaspoon at a time, until no more will dissolve in the water. You have made a solution of epsom salts.

3 Pour some of the solution into a dish, leaving behind any undissolved powder. Put the dish into the refrigerator.

4 Look at the dish every half an hour. After about an hour you should see many needle-like crystals have grown in the dish.

5 Pour away any remaining solution from the dish, and leave the crystals to dry.

6 Look closely at the crystals with a magnifying glass. Can you see the faces and edges of the crystals?

Results
Through a magnifying glass the crystals were seen to have flat faces and straight edges. This shows that their particles are neatly arranged.

What Kinds of Rock Are There?

There are three types of rocks in the Earth's crust. They are **igneous rocks, sedimentary rocks,** and **metamorphic rocks.** The rocks are given these names because of the way they are made. There are many different rocks of each type.

Igneous rocks

Igneous rocks form when red-hot molten rock (called magma) cools down and becomes solid. Sometimes the magma comes out onto the Earth's surface, at volcanoes. At some volcanoes it comes out as runny rock, called lava. At other volcanoes the magma is blasted into tiny bits that fly high into the air and cool to make volcanic ash. Sometimes magma cools underground and turns solid, forming new igneous rock.

Lava flows across Kamoamoa Black Sand Beach on the island of Hawaii. This sort of lava, which forms rounded mounds, is called pahoehoe lava.

Common igneous rocks

Basalt and granite are very common igneous rocks. Basalt is formed at volcanoes when lava cools quite quickly in the air. It is a black rock. Basalt is the most common rock in the Earth's crust. Granite is formed when magma cools slowly underground. It has grains large enough to see.

Recognizing igneous rocks

Examine a sample of rock through a magnifying glass. If you see crystals in different colors interlocked with each other, this normally means the rock is an igneous rock. Igneous rocks do not have flat or wavy layers of rock. They are also strong, and not crumbly like many sedimentary rocks.

This is the Giant's Causeway in Northern Ireland. The rock is basalt that split into six-sided columns as it cooled slowly underground.

Try This!

After runny magma comes out of a volcano's crater, it is called lava. Try this experiment with melted chocolate to see how lava flows and cools.

Prediction

When lava flows down the slopes of a volcano, it slows down as it cools and then goes solid. Also, when lava flows into water, it goes solid more quickly.

Equipment

- cooking chocolate or other plain chocolate
- baking tray
- large pan
- wooden spoon
- large glass bowl (slightly larger than pan so that it will rest inside the pan, but will not touch the bottom of the pan)
- oven glove

This experiment involves using a stove and handling hot pans. Ask an adult to help you.

Method

1 Break up your chocolate into small chunks and put them in a bowl.

2 Pour water into the pan until the water is a couple of inches deep, and put the pan on the stove.

3 Carefully put the bowl inside the pan (the bottom of the bowl must not touch the water), and begin heating the pan.

4 When the water is boiling, steam will come out around the edge of the bowl. Turn down the heat so that the water simmers gently. Stir the chocolate with a wooden spoon until it has all melted.

5 Lift the bowl with an oven glove and pour the chocolate onto one end of a baking tray.

6 Tip up the tray and watch the chocolate slowly flow along it.

7 You can model lava flowing into water too. Prepare another bowl of water. Slowly pour some of the molten chocolate into the water and watch what happens.

Results

The flowing chocolate cools and slowly hardens, forming folds of chocolate. This is a model of how real lava flows and forms new igneous rock. When lava flows into water, the water cools it rapidly, and it solidifies very quickly.

Sedimentary rocks

Sediment is a material made up of millions of small bits of rock that have been deposited in water or by the wind. The sand on a beach is sediment, and so is the mud in an **estuary**. Sedimentary rock is rock that is made up of sediment, but with the pieces of rock joined to each other.

Sediment becomes solid rock when it gets buried under more and more layers of other sediments. Deep underground, under great pressure, the sediment gets squeezed, which makes the particles join together to make rock. This can take millions of years to happen.

Common sedimentary rocks

Common sedimentary rocks include sandstone, mudstone, and limestone. Sandstone is made when sand turns to rock, and mudstone is formed when mud turns to rock. There are several different types of limestone. Most limestones are made up of the skeletons or shells of tiny sea creatures, which fall to the seabed when the creatures die.

The cliffs on the Isle of Hoy in the Orkney Islands, in Scotland, are made of red sandstone. You can see the different layers of sand in the rock.

Recognizing sedimentary rocks

You can often see the pieces of rock (the grains) that make up a piece of sedimentary rock. You might also be able to see layers of different sediments, made up of different-sized pieces of rock, or different-colored pieces of rock. You might also be able to rub the grains off easily.

This sedimentary rock is limestone. The rock is made up of the shells and skeletons of dead sea creatures.

Eureka!

Englishman James Hutton (1726–1797) was the first geologist to realize that sedimentary rocks are made when sediments are buried deep underground. He also realized that rocks on the surface of the Earth are broken down into the sediments that form new rocks.

Rocks from water

Some rocks form from minerals that are dissolved in water. As the water evaporates, or flows over existing rocks, the tiny particles of the minerals in the water join up to make new rock. All these rocks are types of limestone, which is made of a mineral called calcite. The calcite gets into the water when rainwater flows through limestone caves, and slowly dissolves the rock.

This weird and wonderful limestone cave is in Croatia. The needle-like formations are called stalactites, which form as water drips form the cave roof.

Metamorphic rocks

The word "metamorphic" means changing. Metamorphic rocks are made when sedimentary or igneous rocks are changed by pressure and heat deep underground in the Earth's crust. The pressure and heat make the minerals in the rock change into new minerals, and the crystals change size and shape. Common metamorphic rocks are gneiss, schist, marble, and slate.

Recognizing metamorphic rocks

In most metamorphic rocks, such as gneiss and schist, you can see bands of light and dark crystals. This pattern is called foliation. Some metamorphic rocks, such as quartzite and marble, are made up of crystals of just one mineral.

Meteorites

A **meteorite** is a lump of rock not from the Earth but from space. Millions of bits of rock from space hurtle into the Earth's **atmosphere**. But some reach the surface, and these are meteorites. They are bits of rock left over from when the **solar system** was made, or that were thrown into space by collisions between planets and moons.

WHAT'S NEXT?

Astronomers are interested in the rocks that make up the other rocky planets and moons in the solar system. These rocks can tell us about how the solar system formed. **Space probes** to other planets analyze the rocks they find and send data back to Earth. In 2012, the Mars Science Laboratory landed on Mars, carrying instruments to analyze the Martian rocks.

The Leaning Tower of Pisa, in Italy, is constructed from beautiful white marble, which is a metamorphic rock. Much of the world's marble comes from Italy.

How Do Rocks Change?

The surface of the Earth seems like a very solid place to us. But all the time, new rocks are being made, and old rocks are being worn away or turned into different types of rock. Most of these changes take place over millions of years. As the rocks change, the surface of the Earth changes too. For example, new mountains are built up and worn away.

Making new rocks

New igneous rocks are made where magma cools, at volcanoes on the Earth's surface, under the ground, and under the sea. New sedimentary rocks are made underground and under the seabed as layers of sediments are squeezed together.

This is a diagram of how the three types of rock are formed and change into each other. This is called the **rock cycle**.

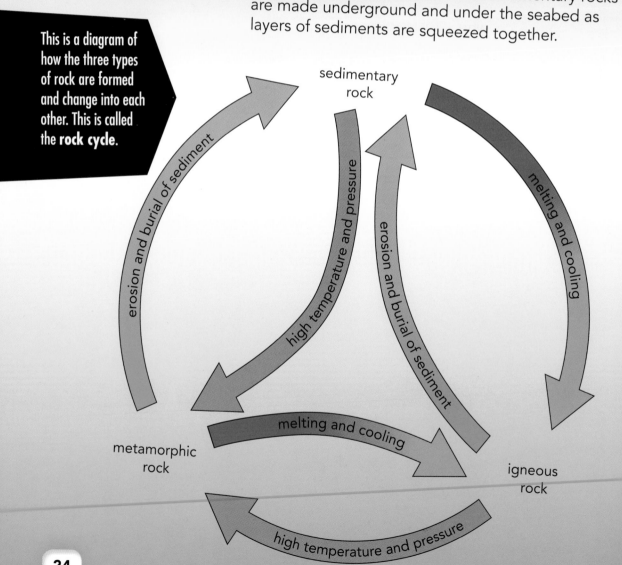

sedimentary rock

erosion and burial of sediment

high temperature and pressure

erosion and burial of sediment

melting and cooling

metamorphic rock

melting and cooling

igneous rock

high temperature and pressure

Destroying rocks

Rocks are broken down by **erosion** (see page 26), which wear away the rocks at the Earth's surface and in caves under the ground. Rocks are always destroyed at some plate boundaries, where rocks at the edges of plates are pushed down into the mantle and melt.

Changing rocks

Sedimentary rocks and igneous rocks are changed into metamorphic rocks, and metamorphic rocks are changed into different metamorphic rocks. These changes happen at plate boundaries, where rocks are squeezed by huge forces, and where the heat of red-hot magma changes the rocks.

Eureka!

Under the world's oceans there is a mountain chain a total of 50,000 miles (80,000 kilometers) long. It's called the Mid-Ocean Ridge system. In 1953, two American geologists, Maurice Ewing and Bruce Heezen, discovered a deep canyon running along the ridge. This showed where tectonic plates are moving apart, and where magma rises to make new rock.

The light-colored mud has been made by erosion of rocks, washed down a river, and deposited here, in the Okavango Delta, Botswana. It may go on to become new sedimentary rock.

Weathering

The weather is one thing that destroys rocks. The hot Sun heats rock in the day, the rock expands slightly, then at night the rock cools and contracts. This gradually weakens the rock, and eventually pieces fall off. Freezing weather also breaks up rock. If water trickles into cracks in rocks, then freezes to make ice, the ice expands and widens the crack. Eventually the rock breaks apart. We call these processes **weathering**. Piles of broken rocks at the bottom of mountains (called scree) are often made by weathering.

The rocky towers of Monument Valley, in Utah, are the remains of a sheet of rock that has been destroyed by weathering and erosion.

Erosion

Erosion is how moving water, the wind, and **glaciers** destroy rocks. Flowing water knocks pieces off rocks as it flows over them. This happens in rivers and at coasts as waves hit the shore. Pieces of rock moved by the water help to smash pieces off the rocks. This is how rivers cut deep river valleys, and how the sea breaks up the seashore. Sand blown along by the wind also erodes rocks, as the particles of sand knock bits off rock they hit. Then the wind blows the bits away. Glaciers gouge (scrape) at rock as they flow slowly down mountains, and carry the rock away.

The bits of rock made by erosion form sediments that might go on to form new sedimentary rock, and also become soils (see pages 28–29).

Pebbles are chunks of rock that have rounded and smoothed by being rubbed and bashed against each other by the power of waves hitting the shore.

DID YOU KNOW?

Chemical weathering happens when rainwater flows over rocks. The water is slightly acidic because it contains dissolved carbon dioxide, and so it dissolves the rock. Limestone dissolves more quickly than other rocks, and chemical weathering creates amazing caves, passages, and weird rock shapes in limestone, which dissolves in water.

Soil

Much of the Earth's landscape is covered with a layer of soil. In some places the soil is just a few inches thick; in others it's many feet deep. Underneath the soil is the top layer of rocks in the crust, known as bedrock. Soil is a mixture of bits of rock and material from plants that have rotted, which is called humus, as well as water and air.

Soil is made by weathering and erosion. Millions of small bits of rock made by weathering and erosion form sediments. Then plants take root in the sediments, and microorganisms and other animals move in.

DID YOU KNOW?

Just 2 pounds (1 kg) of soil (that's about a cupful) contains an amazing number of microorganisms. There may be around 500 billion bacteria, a billion fungi, and 500 million tiny animals.

In this photograph, you can see layers of soil close to a river in New Zealand. The top, dark layer contains living matter such as roots and microorganisms, and dead plant matter.

Living in the soil

Soil is teeming with life. Most organisms in the soil are microorganisms such as bacteria and fungi. These feed on dead plant matter, such as leaves that fall to the ground. Worms, insects, and millipedes also live in the soil. They help to mix the soil and get air into it, which helps plants to grow.

Soils for growing

Soils contain chemicals called nutrients, which plants need in order to grow properly. Nutrients come from rotting plant matter and from rocks. The best soils for growing crops are found alongside rivers and around volcanoes. When rivers flood they bring new sediments, and so new nutrients to the land next to the rivers. Volcanic soils are made from weathered and eroded volcanic rocks.

Valuable soil has been eroded away in this part of Mexico because the trees that hold the soil together have been cut down.

Try This!

Flowing water erodes rock. It also moves sediments from one place to another. Sediments can go on to form sedimentary rocks. Try this experiment to see the power of water at work.

Prediction

When water flows over sediments, it picks up particles and moves them along. When the water slows down, the sediments are left behind.

Equipment

- some play sand
- two old, medium-sized shallow trays (plastic trays or baking trays)
- old cup
- some newspaper
- small plastic box (a few inches high)

Method

1 Cover your working surface with newspaper to protect it in case you spill sand and water.

2 Put two cupfuls of sand onto a tray and spread it out evenly.

3 Put another tray on your work surface, and position the tray with sand so that one corner is over one end of the lower tray. Prop up the opposite corner with a small box so that the tray slopes down from this corner.

4 Fill a cup with water. Now slowly pour water into the upper corner of the sand-filled tray. Water should flow across the upper tray and into the lower tray.

5 Watch what happens to the sand in the lower tray.

Results

The sand in the upper tray is eroded and then deposited on the lower tray. This shows that flowing water moves sediment from one place to another.

What Are Fossils?

Fossils are the imprints of ancient animals and plants that are found in rocks. They are formed when the remains are trapped in sediments and the sediments are turned to rock. Fossils tell us about life on Earth in the distant past.

Forming fossils

Most fossils form when plants or animals are buried quickly by sediments after they die. Normally only the hard parts of animals and plants, such as bones, shells, and woody stems, become fossils. But sometimes the softer parts, such as leaves and feathers, leave a pattern in the sediment before they rot. Animal footprints are sometimes fossilized too. Most fossils are found in limestone and shale. Some sedimentary rocks, such as shelly limestone and chalk, are made up completely of fossils of sea creatures.

A beautiful fossil of part of a fern, which died and was buried in a swamp 270 to 300 million years ago.

Coal

Coal is known as a fossil fuel because it formed over millions of years from the remains of plants. The plants lived in ancient swampy forests, and started to rot as they died. Then they were buried under sediments. Over millions of years underground, the water was squeezed out of them, and they turned into coal.

WHAT'S NEXT?

Fossils of animals and plants that lived millions of years ago are helping scientists to discover more about climate change. The types of animals and plants that lived in different parts of the world are clues to what the climate was like then. They help us to build a picture of how the Earth's climate changed in the past, and how it might change in the future.

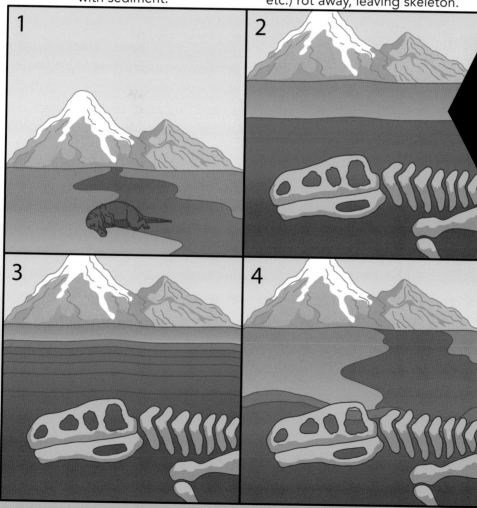

Animal dies and is quickly covered with sediment.

Soft parts of animal (skin, muscle, etc.) rot away, leaving skeleton.

This diagram shows the stages in the formation of a dinosaur fossil.

Minerals in bone change as rock forms.

After millions of years rock is eroded and fossil exposed at surface.

Finding fossils

Fossils appear on the Earth's surface when the layers of sedimentary rocks they are buried under are eroded away. They might have been buried for millions, or even hundreds of millions, of years. When rare fossils are found, paleontologists dig them out with great care. Sometimes fossilized bones can be put together to see what the skeletons of ancient animals looked like.

Paleontologist Luis Chiappe is digging the skull of a protoceratops (a type of plant-eating dinosaur) from the rocks of the Gobi desert in Asia.

DID YOU KNOW?

Fossils are clues to events that happened on Earth millions of years ago. We have found thousands of dinosaur fossils that are more than 65 million years old, but none that is less than 65 million years old. Scientists think that much of life on Earth, including all the dinosaurs, was wiped out when a huge meteorite hit the Earth.

What fossils tell us

Nearly everything we know about life on Earth in the distant past comes from fossils. We know about the different animals and plants, and when they lived. And we know when different animals began living on the Earth, and when they died out. Without fossils, we wouldn't know that animals such as the dinosaurs ever lived.

Eureka!

In 1861, fossils of a chicken-sized animal with feathers were discovered in the region of Bavaria in Germany. The fossils are about 150 million years old. The new animal was given the name Archaeopteryx. It has some of the features of a bird and some of the features of a dinosaur. It may have been the very first type of bird.

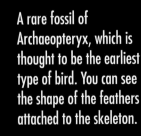

A rare fossil of Archaeopteryx, which is thought to be the earliest type of bird. You can see the shape of the feathers attached to the skeleton.

How Do We Use Rocks?

Rock is an important material because of its properties. We use hard rocks for making things, from houses to ornaments, and soft rock such as clay for making pottery. We get all the metals we need from rocks, and many useful minerals too.

These ancient cutting tools were made tens of millions of years ago by chipping away at pieces of flint. They were found in Austria.

Early rock tools

Rock was one of the first materials that humans used, along with wood and animal skins and bones. Flint was the most useful sort of rock. Archaeologists have found flint tools that people used tens of thousands of years ago for cutting up the animals they hunted and for shaping wood. This period in history is known as the Stone Age.

Rock for building

Rocks are used all over the world as a building material. The best building rock is rock that is easy to cut and shape but that doesn't crumble and stands up to weathering. Clay is a very soft rock that gets very hard when it is heated in a kiln. It is molded into shape to make bricks and tiles. Concrete is made from rock too. It contains **cement**, which is made from limestone, and gravel or crushed rock. Road surfaces are also made from crushed rock.

WHAT'S NEXT?

Some of the other planets in the solar system, their moons, and **asteroids** are all made of rock. These rocks may contain minerals that don't exist on Earth, and elements that are very rare on Earth. Mining companies are making plans to send robots to these other worlds to find and bring back these materials.

Buildings such as this mill in Ireland are often made of locally available rock cut into blocks and cemented together. Here the roof is made of clay tiles.

Metals from rocks

Most of the metals we use today come from rock in the Earth's crust. They include iron (which is used to make steel), aluminum, and copper. These are all chemical elements, and they are all contained in minerals found in rocks. The minerals we get metals from are called metal ores. For example, the main ore from which we get aluminum is called bauxite, and the main ore of iron is hematite. The first stage in producing metals is to dig the ores out of the ground, in mines and quarries, and sometimes by dredging them from the seabed.

DID YOU KNOW?

Small chunks of gold called nuggets are found in some sediments of gravel and sand. They can be found using a method called panning. The gravel is swirled around in a shallow pan so that gold, which is heavier than the rock pieces, falls to the bottom.

Getting metals out

Different methods are used to get metals from their ores. For example, to get aluminum from bauxite, the bauxite is molten and then electricity is passed through it. This removes the aluminum. To get iron from hematite, the hematite is heated and the oxygen is removed to leave molten iron. This process is called smelting.

Native metals

A few metals are found in rocks as elements. They are not part of minerals. They include gold, silver, and platinum. This is why gold was one of first metals to be discovered, thousands of years ago.

Eureka!

Ten thousand years ago, the only materials people knew how to use were wood, stone, and animal skins and bones. Metals were discovered one by one by accident. First was copper, discovered about 5000 BCE. Later, copper was mixed with tin to make bronze. Iron was discovered by about 500 BCE.

Iron comes from iron ore. The ore is heated with carbon in a blast furnace. This releases the iron from the ore, and molten iron is poured out.

Rock for decoration

Rocks are cut into slabs and polished smooth to give a beautiful finish. They are used as decorative stone on the floors and walls of buildings, and for worktops and table tops in kitchens. As well as being attractive to look at, they are strong and long-lasting. Sculptors cut and shape rock to make sculptures, and practical objects such as vases and containers.

Marble can be cut and carved into intricate shapes such as the top of this column.

Marble

Marble is a very popular decorative stone, especially for floor tiles and wall tiles, and for sculpture. Marble is limestone that has been changed by heat and pressure deep underground. It comes in a huge variety of colors and patterns. The finest and most expensive marble comes from Italy.

Gemstones

Rubies, emeralds, sapphires, and diamonds are examples of gemstones. They are minerals found in rocks that are beautiful because of their color, but are also very rare, and very durable. Their main use is in jewelry, when they are cut and polished. Some have other uses, such as diamonds for drills and rubies for lasers. Other gemstones are more common. Examples are agate (a mineral that contains beautiful rings of color), jasper, and amethyst.

DID YOU KNOW?

The process that creates limestone caves underground **erodes** limestone and marble used for building, decoration, and sculpture. Rain is slightly acidic, and it dissolves the rock. Over many years the surface of the rock is eroded and the decoration or sculpture spoiled. Where there is air pollution, the acid is stronger and more damaging.

This bright green mineral is garnet uvarovite. The crystals are too small to be used for gemstones, but pieces can be polished to make decorative stones.

What Have We Learned About Rocks?

Rocks are the materials that make up the Earth's crust—the outer layer of the Earth. Minerals are materials that rocks are made of.

There are three types of rock, which are sedimentary rocks, igneous rocks, and metamorphic rocks. Sedimentary rocks are made up of layers of sediments, such as sand and mud, that have been buried deep underground. Igneous rocks are made when molten rock cools. Metamorphic rocks are made when rocks are changed by immense heat and pressure. Rocks are always being made, changed, and destroyed. This is known as the rock cycle.

There are spectacular rock formations all over the world. This is Sugar Loaf Mountain in Rio de Janeiro, Brazil, which is the solid core of an extinct volcano.

Rocks tell us about the animals and plants that lived on Earth long before because they contain fossils. In fact, we only know that they existed because of fossils.

Rocks and minerals are useful materials. We use rocks as building materials, get the metals we need from minerals, and use fossil fuels for power. We couldn't live our modern lives without rocks. We depend on them like the people who lived in the Stone Age, tens of thousands of years ago.

WHAT'S NEXT?

Now that you know a little about rocks and minerals, you could start your own rock, mineral, and fossil collection. Perhaps you could collect pebbles from a stony beach, where you might find many different types of rocks. Make a note of where and when you found the rocks. Never take rocks from sensitive areas such as nature reserves or important geological sites. You can often find mineral specimens for sale.

Museums often have collections of interesting rocks and minerals, such as these strange fluorescent minerals.

Glossary

asteroid large piece of rock smaller than a planet that orbits the Sun

astronomer scientist who studies space and the objects in space

atmosphere the layer of air that surrounds the Earth

cement material made with lime from limestone and clay, used to make mortar and concrete

concrete construction material that is made with cement, water, sand, and gravel

continent large body of land on the Earth's surface (there are seven continents)

crust the solid outer layer of the Earth, which is made of solid rock

crystal material in which the particles are arranged in neat rows and columns, so they are neatly packed together

element substance made of atoms that cannot be broken down into simpler substances

erosion wearing away of a surface by the weather, flowing water, waves, and so on

estuary the lowest section of a river, where the river meets the sea

evaporate to change from a liquid to a gas

fossil remains of an ancient plant or animal found in rock

geologist scientist who studies the rocks of the Earth's crust

glacier body of ice that flows slowly downhill, like a river of ice

gravel material made up of numerous small stones, which can be rounded or jagged

igneous rock rock formed when molten rock (magma or lava) cools and solidifies

magma molten rock under or in the Earth's crust

metamorphic rock type of rock formed when rocks are changed by heat and pressure, normally deep underground

meteorite piece of rock from space that enters the Earth's atmosphere and hits the Earth's surface

mineral one of many solid, nonliving materials that makes up rocks

plate boundary line along which two tectonic plates meet

rock cycle process in which new rocks are continuously made and old rocks are continuously destroyed or changed into new rocks

sediment material made from numerous small pieces of rock, or numerous shells or skeletons of sea creatures

sedimentary rock type of rock formed from layers of sediment (which may be particles of rock or the shells or skeletons of sea creatures)

solar system the Sun, the planets and their moons, and other material that orbits the Sun

space probe spacecraft sent from Earth to visit other objects (such as planets or moons) in the solar system

tectonic plate one of the many large pieces that the Earth's crust is cracked into

volcano place where magma comes out onto the Earth's surface, or a mountain formed from solidified lava and ash

weathering breaking down of rock by the action of the weather (such as hot and cold, or ice)

Find Out More

Books

Davis, Barbara J. *Minerals, Rocks, and Soil* (Sci-Hi: Earth Science). Chicago: Heinemann-Raintree, 2009.

Hurd, Will. *Investigating Rocks* (Do It Yourself). Chicago: Heinemann Library, 2010.

Oxlade, Chris. *Sedimentary Rocks* (Let's Rock). Chicago: Heinemann-Raintree, 2012.

Rice, William B. *Rocks and Minerals* (Mission: Science). Mankato, Minn.: Compass Point, 2008.

Woolley, Alan. *Spotter's Guides: Rocks and Minerals.* Eveleth, Minn.: Usborne Publishing, 2007.

Web sites

www.mineralogy4kids.org
You can learn more about crystals, the minerals in your house, and the properties of minerals, as well as play some games at this site run by the Mineralogical Society of America.

http://mineralsciences.si.edu
This site explores the "Mineral Sciences" section of the web site of the Smithsonian Institution.

www.onegeology.org/extra/kids/rocks_and_minerals.html
Learn more about rocks and minerals from Larry limestone at this site run by OneGeology, an international project making geological map data of the Earth accessible.

http://volcano.oregonstate.edu/oldroot/education/vwlessons/lessons/Slideshow/Slideindex.html
See pictures of samples of various minerals and rocks at this web site.

Places to visit

The Natural History Museum in Los Angeles, California, has a Gem and Mineral Hall with over 2,000 specimens of gems and minerals from all over the world.

You can investigate physical science topics at the Museum of Science and Industry in Chicago.

The Exploratorium, in San Francisco, examines many different aspects of science and offers hands-on activities.

The Museum of Life and Science in Durham, North Carolina, has hands-on activities that take visitors through the process of using scientific tools and conducting scientific inquiry. And you can watch real scientists as they conduct their research!

The Earth & Mineral Science Museum at The Pennsylvania State University in State College, Pennsylvania, has numerous fine minerals on display, as well as mining and scientific equipment.

At the Science Museum of Minnesota, in St. Paul, you can carry out science experiments!

Further research

There's lots more to find out about rocks and minerals. Here are some ideas for further research:

What rocks make up the landscape where you live? You can often find the answer in your local museum, which may have a geological display.

Where are rocks and minerals used around your home, and in your area? Look at utensils and ornaments in your home and backyard, and at other local buildings. Can you identify any of the rocks and minerals? A simple field guide to rocks and minerals will help.

Index